Roman
Britain

Alex Woolf

W
FRANKLIN WATTS
LONDON · SYDNEY

First published in 2006 by
Franklin Watts
338 Euston Road
London NW1 3BH

Franklin Watts Australia
Hachette Children's Books
Level 17/207 Kent Street
Sydney NSW 2000

ISBN-10: 0 7496 6466 5
ISBN-13: 978 0 7496 6466 4
Dewey Classification: 720.9

Planning and production by
Discovery Books Limited
Editor: Helen Dwyer
Design: Simon Borrough
Picture Research: Rachel Tisdale

A CIP catalogue record for this book is available
from the British Library.

Printed in China

Photo credits:
Front (and back) cover all pictures Discovery
Picture Library/Alex Ramsay, title page Alex
Ramsay, page 4 top & bottom Discovery Picture
Library/Alex Ramsay, 5 top Discovery Picture
Library/Robert Humphrey, 5 bottom & 6 top
Discovery Picture Library/Alex Ramsay, 6 bottom
National Museum of Wales/Evan Chapman, 7 top
Barcombe Villa, 7 bottom National Museum of
Wales/Richard Brewer, 8 CADW, 9 top English
Heritage/Ivan Lapper, 9 bottom Discovery
Picture Library/Alex Ramsay, 10 Dorset County
Council, 11 top National Museum of Wales/
Penny Hill, 11 bottom Kent Archaeological
Rescue Unit, 12 CADW, 13 top CADW/John
Banbury, 13 bottom CADW, 14 top National
Museum of Wales/ Evan Chapman, 14 bottom &
15 top Discovery Picture Library/Alex Ramsay,
15 bottom Exeter Archaeology, 16 top CADW,
16 bottom CADW/John Banbury, 17 top
Discovery Picture Library/Alex Ramsay, 17
bottom Alamy/ Ian Murray, 18 Newport City
Council, 19 top Chester City Council, 19
bottom Discovery Picture Library/Alex Ramsay,
20 top St Albans Museums, 20 bottom Discovery
Picture Library/Alex Ramsay, 21 top National
Trust Picture Library/Ian Shaw, 21 bottom
Fishbourne Roman Palace/Sussex Archaeological
Society, 22 Discovery Picture Library/Alex
Ramsay, 23 top & bottom left Discovery Picture
Library/Alex Ramsay, 23 bottom right Fishbourne
Roman Palace/Sussex Archaeological Society, 24
Discovery Picture Library/Alex Ramsay, 25 top
Heritage Trail, 25 bottom Discovery Picture
Library/Alex Ramsay, 26 National Museum of
Wales/Richard Brewer, 27 top, 27 bottom & 28
Discovery Picture Library/Alex Ramsay, 29 top
Alex Ramsay, 29 bottom Stewart Ross

CONTENTS

ROMAN INVASION

In 43 CE, Britain was invaded by the Romans (a people who first came from the city of Rome in Italy) and became a province of their huge empire. At its height, the Roman Empire covered most of Europe, as well as parts of northern Africa, western Asia and the Middle East.

Changing Britain

To control their newly won territory, the Romans built heavily defended forts around the country. These forts were linked to each other by a network of sturdy roads. Most famously of all, on the northern edge of their British territory, the Romans built a coast-to-coast wall (below) to protect the province from the tribes who lived in Caledonia (Scotland).

Hadrian's Wall was built on the orders of the Roman emperor Hadrian. Construction began in 122 CE and it took 14 years to complete. Hadrian's Wall was the largest structure ever made by the Romans.

Roman roads were built to last. In fact, many are still used today. This Roman road in Lancashire is now used as a footpath.

The Romans built temples in every town they established in Britain. Here are the ruins of a Roman-built temple at Caerwent in Monmouthshire.

Great builders

The Romans were excellent builders and engineers. In Britain, as well as in every other part of their empire, they built great towns, with public squares, town halls and shops. They also built Roman-style entertainment centres, including bath-houses, theatres and amphitheatres. They constructed ornate temples to both Roman and local British gods, and in the countryside they built large, luxurious houses called villas.

Roman remains

The Romans finally left Britain in 410 CE, because their troops were needed to defend against attacks on other parts of their empire. Although the Romans had been in Britain for almost 400 years, most traces of their culture disappeared soon afterwards. All that remained were their extraordinary buildings and structures, many of which can be seen to this day.

AQUEDUCTS

Roman towns had bath-houses, fountains and sewer systems, so they required lots of water. The Romans achieved this by building clay- or wood-lined pipes and channels that could carry water over very long distances. These pipes were called aqueducts. Remains of Roman aqueducts have been found at Dorchester, Wroxeter, Gloucester, Exeter and Lincoln.

Evidence of the sturdiness of Roman building techniques can be seen in the remains of this Roman-built fort at Burgh castle, Norfolk. The walls are almost three metres thick at the base and stand five metres high.

DISCOVERING ROMAN BUILDINGS

We can learn a great deal about life in Roman Britain by studying the remains of Roman buildings. A few structures have been known about ever since Roman times. However, most Roman remains were built over after the Romans had gone. They had to be rediscovered many centuries later through excavation by archaeologists.

Archaeologists excavate the site of the Roman villa at Chedworth in Gloucestershire. A total of 32 rooms were discovered, with well-preserved remains of mosaics and baths.

Understanding sites

Once excavated, the sites are not always easy to understand. Most consist of little more than building foundations and the remains of walls showing the layout of different rooms. From this, archaeologists try to work out what the building must have looked like.

KEY MOMENTS IN ROMAN-BRITISH ARCHAEOLOGY

1847 Roman theatre at Verulamium (St Albans) discovered.

1864 Chedworth Villa in Gloucestershire found.

1939 Roman villa unearthed at Lullingstone in Kent.

1945–7 Two Roman shrines excavated on Scargill Moor, County Durham.

1954 Temple to the god Mithras discovered in London.

1960 The Roman palace at Fishbourne discovered by accident during the digging of a water mains trench.

1987 Parts of a Roman amphitheatre discovered under Guildhall Yard, London.

Excavation of the granaries (grain stores) in the fortress at Usk in Monmouthshire. The horizontal lines are the foundations for the timber granaries, with the holes for vertical posts visible in the base. The vertical lines are unexcavated areas.

One way to make sense of Roman building remains is to compare them with better-preserved examples from elsewhere in the Roman Empire. This is possible because the Romans tended to use the same basic design for many of their buildings, such as bath-houses, temples and town halls.

Dating sites

Another problem in understanding sites is that many Roman buildings were taken over by later peoples who adapted them for their own purposes. Archaeologists must therefore find out which parts of a site are Roman and which parts are not.

There are various ways of dating sites. For example, if a coin is found buried inside building material it was probably dropped by the builders so you can work out the approximate date of the building.

The remains of a wall at Barcombe villa in East Sussex. The striped rod is a ranging pole, which is used to demonstrate the size of an excavation to people looking at photographs.

Archaeologists can learn a lot from inscriptions on excavated buildings. The one pictured on the left was found in the ruins of Gelligaer fort in south Wales and tells us that the fort was constructed between 103 and 111 CE.

Aerial views

In some cases, Roman settlements are better understood by studying them from the air. In the countryside, a Roman road or stone floor can cause crops growing above it to wither because it prevents water from getting to their roots. This makes a crop mark. The street plan of Roman Silchester in Hampshire can clearly be seen by looking at crop marks from the air.

ROMAN TOWNS

Before the Romans arrived, there were no towns in Britain, just small tribal settlements and hill forts. Some Roman towns, including Colchester, Lincoln and Gloucester, began as military bases. Others, such as St Albans, were built by the Romans on top of older settlements. Still others were built by Britons who imitated the Roman way of life and constructed new towns in the Roman style, including Silchester, Cirencester and Exeter.

Town walls

Roman towns were at first protected by earth defences, which were later replaced by stone. At intervals along the walls large projecting towers called bastions made the walls easier to defend.

SEE FOR YOURSELF
The remains of Roman towns can be found in many parts of Britain, including:
1 York, North Yorkshire
2 Lincoln
3 Wroxeter, Shropshire
4 Leicester
5 Colchester, Essex
6 Gloucester
7 St Albans, Hertfordshire
8 Cirencester, Gloucestershire
9 Caerwent, Monmouthshire
10 London
11 Silchester, Hampshire
12 Bath, Somerset
13 Exeter, Devon

The stone walls seen here, surrounding the Roman town of Caerwent, Monmouthshire, were built in about 330 CE and in places they still rise to a height of five metres.

Grid system

Throughout their empire, the Romans built towns in exactly the same style. They were designed in the form of a grid, with streets built at right-angles to each other between rectangular blocks of buildings known as insulae (islands). On these insulae were the town's private houses, shops and public buildings. You can see the grid pattern of the streets of Roman Silchester in this painting (right).

Streets and buildings

The streets of Roman towns were between five and eight metres wide. Their width depended on their importance. They had a gravel surface and were sloped at each side for drainage. Most of the buildings were originally made of wood. Later they were rebuilt in brick. Occasionally, more ornate, stone structures were built, such as the temples at Bath and Colchester.

A reconstruction of Roman Silchester. You can see the grid system of streets surrounded by a defensive wall. In the centre are the public square and town hall, and just outside the town is the circular amphitheatre.

Near the centre of the Roman town of Viroconium (Wroxeter) was a large public bath-house. Here are the remains of the furnace that was used to heat the water.

Town Houses

Most town houses were originally built of wood, or had a timber frame filled with clay. Many of these were later rebuilt in long-lasting brick. The simplest town houses were long, narrow rectangular buildings with four or five rooms. Wealthier town-dwellers lived in larger homes, which often had two wings arranged in an L shape.

Expanding homes

The grandest town houses had three or four wings surrounding a central garden or courtyard. As their wealth grew, these richer residents may have wanted to increase their living space. With no ground space to expand into, they built upwards. Many British town houses had two storeys.

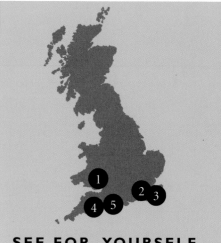

SEE FOR YOURSELF
Remains of these grander Roman town houses can still be seen.
1 Pound Lane, Caerwent, Monmouthshire
2 Butchery Lane, Canterbury
3 Roman Painted House, Dover
4 Catherine Street, Exeter
5 Colliton Park, Dorchester, Dorset

This fourth-century Roman town house at Dorchester was excavated in the 1930s. It features some interesting mosaics with geometric patterns, a column and a well. Roofs and walls have been added in recent times to protect the Roman remains.

Luxurious living

By the third century CE luxurious features were added to the wealthier homes, such as mosaic floors, finely painted walls (right), hypocausts (see page 15) and sometimes even private bath-houses.

Glass windows

Glass-making was introduced to Britain by the Romans, who had learned the skill from peoples of north Africa. Glass-making was an expensive process and only the very rich could afford glazed windows. Although most Roman glass was coloured and not very transparent, it did at least allow light to enter rooms, while keeping out the often cold British weather.

Homes as shops

Many of the simpler town houses were businesses too. The room facing the street would often be open at the front and serve as a shop during the day. Then the shutters would be closed, and the shop would become a workroom at night. Living rooms were at the back of these buildings. There were usually just two or three rooms where a family lived, ate and slept. There were no separate kitchens and bathrooms in these houses.

This painting of a peacock was found on the wall of a third-century town house in Caerwent, south Wales. The blue and red paints used in the picture were luxury items, imported from distant parts of the empire. They suggest that the house was owned by someone rich and important.

Part of a Roman roof tile found in Dover. There are two types of Roman roof tile. Tegulae, such as the one pictured here, were flat, rectangular pieces with raised sides. Imbrices were semi-circular and sat on the ridge of a building.

THE TOWN CENTRE

At the heart of every Roman town was a large public square, known as the forum. This was usually at the junction of two major roads. Next to the forum was the basilica, which was the town hall and law court.

Forum

The forum was an important gathering place where people could meet, shop, eat and exchange news. The basilica took up one side of the forum. Around the other three sides was a covered walkway, supported by pillars, containing shops and eating places. Above the shops there was usually a second storey containing storerooms and offices.

The Roman town of Caerwent in Monmouthshire contains one of the best-preserved examples of a forum and basilica in Britain.

A reconstruction showing how the Caerwent forum and basilica might have looked in Roman times.

Basilica

The basilica was made up of a great hall, with a row of offices and chambers at the back. The hall usually had a central area and two wings separated by two rows of columns. At the end of the hall were semicircular courtrooms where judges dealt with crimes and disputes. Elsewhere in the basilica were offices for local administration.

Shops

The streets leading off the forum were lined with shops. Here, blacksmiths, carpenters, drapers, pottery and glassware vendors, wine merchants and bakers all competed for customers. The shops varied in size from single rooms to larger buildings with storerooms and living quarters behind the shop. Their narrow fronts were all open to the street.

Market halls

Some of the larger towns, including Wroxeter, St Albans and Cirencester, also had a permanent market hall where traders could rent shop space. The market halls stood near the centre of town, close to the forum. Each one contained around 12 shops.

CHEATING THE CUSTOMERS?

Roman shopkeepers used weights to measure out food for their customers. Weights have been found at St Albans, many of which are inaccurate. Was this accidental or were the shopkeepers trying to cheat the public? It is impossible to say for sure, although we have a clue: one of the rooms of the St Albans market hall may have been occupied by the local weights and measures office, whose job was to check the accuracy of shopkeepers' weights.

Excavated shops in Pound Lane, Caerwent. They were first built in 150 CE, and further developed over the next 200 years.

BATH-HOUSES

One of the most important meeting places in a Roman town was the bath-house. A visit to the baths was both a chance to meet friends and an opportunity to bathe and exercise.

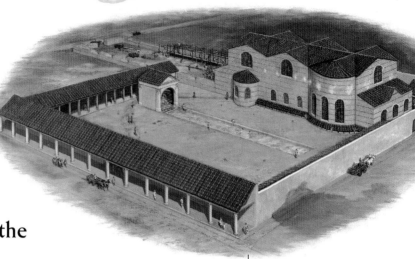

The bath-house complex

Bath-houses were large complexes with changing rooms, exercise halls and three separate bathing rooms – the frigidarium (cold room), tepidarium (warm room) and caldarium (hot room). Bath-houses had elaborate heating systems, provided by an underground furnace that heated the water and the under-floor space.

The greatest example of a Roman bath-house in Britain is at Bath (right). It was known by the Romans as Aquae Sulis (Waters of Sulis). Sulis was a British god.

A reconstruction of the bath-house complex at the Roman fortress of Caerleon in south-east Wales as it might have looked in about 80 CE. Next to the bath-house is an outdoor exercise area and a covered walkway.

PAST TO PRESENT

The Great Bath at Aquae Sulis (left) originally had a timber roof, but this was replaced in the second century by a heavier roof that required much thicker pillars to support it. This is why the pillar bases you can see today project into the bath itself.

The gap in the middle of the Old Work (the high wall in the background) at Wroxeter in Shropshire was an arched entrance containing double doors that opened onto a large exercise hall. The walls in the foreground divided the different rooms of the bath-house.

SEE FOR YOURSELF

Remains of Roman baths in Britain can be seen in the following places:
1 Ravenglass, Cumbria
2 Wroxeter, Shropshire
3 Wall, near Lichfield, Staffordshire
4 Caerleon, Newport
5 Bath, Somerset

Wroxeter

The remains of the bath-house at Wroxeter (the Roman town of Viroconium) include an eight-metre-high section of wall (above). This originally formed part of one side of the bath-house. During Roman times, up to 1,000 people at a time could enjoy its facilities.

The hypocaust

The Romans provided their bath-houses and other buildings with an under-floor heating system known as a hypocaust. Beneath the floor was an empty space supported at regular intervals by brick or stone pillars, like those at Exeter pictured on the right. A furnace at one end of the room would create heat that circulated in the space under the floor. Flues in the walls would carry the heat to rooms above. In a bath-house, the caldarium would be placed nearest the furnace, and the frigidarium would be furthest from the heat.

The remains of the hypocaust, or under-floor heating system, at the bath-house of the Roman fortress at Exeter.

15

TEMPLES

The Romans and Romanized British built many temples in which they worshipped both Roman and British gods and goddesses. More than 50 Roman-British temple sites have been found in towns and country areas.

Roman-British temples, such as the one pictured on the right, were generally modest in size, intended to hold just a few worshippers at any one time. However, there were some very grand ones built, for example at Bath and Colchester.

The remains of a Roman-British temple at Caerwent in Monmouthshire. The square-shaped temple had walls about 60 centimetres thick, an apse (a semi-circular projection) to the north and a portico (a covered entrance) to the south.

Temple layout

The temples were mostly square, although some were round or polygonal. They were surrounded by a veranda or covered walkway. Inside was a shrine where people could sacrifice animals or leave offerings to the gods. The interiors often had painted walls and mosaic floors, and some had tall columns to either side of the entrance.

A reconstruction of the temple at Caerwent. It was built to honour Mars-Ocelus, a combination of the Roman war god Mars and the British warrior god Ocelus.

The remains of the temple to the god Mithras at Carrawburgh, near Hadrian's Wall. In Roman times the walls, benches and altars would have been painted with colourful scenes. Fragments of painted wall plaster were found during the excavation. You can see a reconstruction of this temple as it was in Roman times in the Museum of Antiquities at the University of Newcastle-upon-Tyne.

PAST TO PRESENT

The temple of Emperor Claudius at Colchester was later incorporated into Colchester Castle, built in the 11th century. It is still possible to visit the Roman vaults beneath the castle. The vault walls are around 1.5 metres thick. The photo shows fragments from the Roman temple, stored in the vaults of the castle.

The cult of Mithras

Alongside the worship of traditional Roman and British gods, several deities (gods and goddesses) from more distant lands also had their followers in Britain. One god who was particularly popular with the Roman army was Mithras, the Persian god of light and truth. Five temples to Mithras have been found in Britain. Four are near forts, and one is in London.

The temples to Mithras were all built to a common design. They were stone-built rectangular buildings with timber roofs. A small, outer room led to the inner temple containing a central area with raised benches against each wall. In the picture of the temple at Carrawburgh (above), you can see the edges of the central area marked by timber posts. At the far end archaeologists found a statue of Mithras slaying a bull.

AMPHITHEATRES AND OTHER THEATRES

At the edges of many Roman towns and military bases, amphitheatres were built to stage popular shows.

Bloodthirsty

These shows were usually bloodthirsty and began with the baiting and slaughter of wild animals. This was followed by battles to the death between trained fighters known as gladiators, or sometimes between the gladiators and wild animals. Female professional fighters called gladiatrice may also have participated, though very rarely.

Typical arenas

Amphitheatres were usually oval-shaped, with a sand-covered central arena surrounded by tiers of wooden seats. The seats were placed on earth banks supported by timber. In continental Europe, amphitheatres were often built of stone.

Caerleon

One of the largest and best preserved amphitheatres in Britain is at the Roman fort of Caerleon in south Wales, pictured above. There were eight entrances to the arena. These included two major entrances (at the top and bottom of this photo) used for processions and six smaller ones used by spectators. Caerleon amphitheatre probably seated around 6,000 people.

The amphitheatre at Caerleon. The oval arena is 56 metres long and 41.5 metres wide. The bank of earth between the inner and outer walls supported rows of wooden seating. The outer wall was just under two metres thick.

Military amphitheatres

Amphitheatres near forts, such as Chester (above) and Richborough in Kent, were used as much by soldiers for drill and weapons training as they were for games. Their arenas had to be larger than the arenas of those used just for entertainment.

Smaller theatres

Very few smaller theatres were built in Britain, probably because the Britons liked the rough entertainment of the games, which needed a lot of space. Theatre remains have been found at St Albans in Hertfordshire, Canterbury in Kent and Gosbecks in Essex. They were D-shaped buildings, with semi-circular banks of seats facing a raised stage. The picture below shows the theatre at St Albans. You can see the steep earth banks where rows of wooden seats were placed.

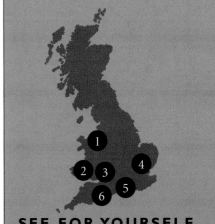

SEE FOR YOURSELF

Theatre remains can be found at:
1 Chester, Cheshire
2 Carmarthen, Wales
3 Caerleon, Wales
4 St Albans, Hertfordshire
5 Chichester, Sussex
6 Dorchester, Dorset

The open-air theatre at Verulamium (St Albans) was built in about 140 CE, near the town centre. It could seat up to 2,000 people.

Villas

The wealthy elite of Roman Britain built elegant country houses called villas. These were not simply homes, but lay at the heart of working farms and contained offices and farm buildings.

Different styles

The simplest design was a small, rectangular building, often timber framed, with five or six interconnecting rooms. A second, larger type of villa had a row of separate rooms for eating, sleeping, entertaining, bathing and cooking. Each room had its own door, opening onto a long corridor that ran the length of the villa. A third type of villa had a long central space flanked by two rows of interior pillars. Living quarters were usually located along the side walls.

The grandest villas were more elaborate, with two or three wings arranged around a rectangular courtyard. The grandest, like Chedworth (below), even had a fourth wing, completely enclosing the courtyard.

The flint and chalk foundations of a Roman villa at Wheathampstead, Hertfordshire. The villa had ten rooms including a corridor running along the south side (the front of this picture), possibly with a central entrance. The two narrow rooms to either side of the large central room may have been staircases.

You can see the position of the courtyard and surrounding walls in this photo taken at Chedworth villa in Gloucestershire. The buildings with roofs are modern ones to protect rooms containing mosaics. All the remaining walls have been topped with stone slabs to prevent them being worn away.

MOSAIC FLOORS

The Romans introduced the art of the mosaic to Britain. To make a mosaic, the craftsperson cut up coloured stones into small pieces called tesserae, arranged them to form patterns, and then fixed them to a bed of cement. This was difficult and time-consuming work. Some of the best mosaic floors in Britain can be found at villas such as Lullingstone, Bignor, Woodchester and Chedworth. The photo on the right shows part of the mosaic in the dining room at Chedworth. The figure, representing winter, wears a hooded cloak and holds a dead hare and a leafless branch.

Luxurious living

The largest villas had beautifully decorated rooms with mosaic floors, painted walls and glazed windows. The villa at Fishbourne in West Sussex is the biggest ever found in Britain. It was probably designed by a top architect brought in from Rome. The remains of the north wing include richly decorated mosaic floors.

Below is a model of Fishbourne villa. It boasted a huge reception hall, a 24-metre-long assembly room, a bath complex and several courtyards. In total, the villa had 160 stone columns and 50 mosaic floors.

GARDENS

Many of the larger Roman villas had a garden. These were carefully landscaped spaces, designed to enchant and relax those who visited them. Gardens were usually situated in a courtyard, bordered by rooms such as the triclinium, the room where guests were entertained.

Some Roman town houses had small courtyard gardens. Archaeologists have recreated this one in Cirencester.

Garden features

The grandest gardens had many features, including lawns, hedges, flower beds, shrubs, trees and statues. People could wander along broad gravel paths and trellised walkways or sit on marble seats. Piped water fed ornamental stone fountains and fish ponds.

However, Roman gardens were not designed purely for pleasure. Many edible and medicinal plants were grown in gardens excavated at Silchester in Hampshire. They included vegetables such as garlic, rhubarb, lettuce, cabbage, cucumber and plantain, and herbs such as coriander and St John's wort.

Fishbourne

One of the biggest gardens in Roman Britain was at the villa at Fishbourne near Chichester (see page 21). There were actually two gardens there. One was a formal garden created in a large courtyard more than 90 metres across, surrounded by the rooms of the house. The other was an even larger, more naturally landscaped space on an artificial terrace to the south.

The formal garden had lawns and trees carefully placed for the view they provided from the house. Its beds contained plants such as roses and lilies. Hedges were grown in elaborate patterns. Underground pipes fed the fountains and basins.

This stone drainage gutter excavated at Fishbourne ran between the wall of the villa and the garden.

Archaeologists have been able to recreate the garden at Fishbourne (left) by studying tree pits, and bedding trenches where hedges grew (above).

ROADS

The Romans built more than 16,000 kilometres of well-made roads, linking every fort and town in Britain. These roads made the tasks of administering Britain and putting down rebellions much easier.

Features of roads

To enable their troops and supplies to move swiftly around the country, the Romans built their roads as straight as possible, often going over hills rather than around them.

Roman roads were between four and nine metres wide, depending on their importance. All roads had rounded tops that allowed water to drain away to the sides.

However, road-building techniques varied, depending on local conditions and available materials. Most roads consisted of a foundation of large stones and a surface of gravel, pressed down and mixed with small stones and earth for smoothness. Occasionally, roads had paved surfaces, such as the one at Blackstone Edge in Lancashire (above).

This is part of what remains of the paved Roman road at Blackstone Edge, Lancashire. The sturdy gutter at the kerb helps with drainage.

Sometimes roads were raised on a bank of earth or clay and rubble to help troops spot an enemy ambush. Roads across marshy ground were built on top of a framework of tree trunks and flat stones. When roads crossed rivers the Romans had to build bridges. None of these survive in Britain but the ends of a bridge can still be seen near Chesters Fort on Hadrian's Wall (right).

Milestones

The Romans placed milestones along their main roads, marking every Roman mile (1,480 metres). They were inscribed with the name of the nearest town and the distance to it in miles. Milestones were cylindrical stones, up to 1.8 metres tall. Almost 100 Roman milestones survive today, including the one at Chesterholm in Northumberland pictured below.

The remains of the eastern end of a Roman bridge that once crossed the North Tyne River. The original bridge, built around 120 CE, was rebuilt on a much larger scale in about 220 CE. Nearly 60 metres in length, it consisted of four arches supported by three massive piers.

This milestone at Chesterholm was set up to help Roman travellers and messengers find their way between towns and forts along Hadrian's Wall.

PAST TO PRESENT

Many modern roads continue to follow the old Roman routes. For example, much of Watling Street, which ran from the Kent coast to Wroxeter, is now under the A2, A5 and M1. Ermine Street, which connected London and York, is still traceable on modern road maps.

FORTS

The Romans established military control over Britain by building a network of forts up and down the country. They provided permanent bases for auxiliary units (groups of soldiers who were not Roman citizens). There were also three legionary fortresses – at Caerleon, Chester and York. Each of these was large enough to hold an entire legion (about 6,000 troops, who were all Roman citizens).

Defences

Most forts were rectangular in shape with rounded corners. The early forts were surrounded by a ditch and a turf or clay embankment, which was topped with a timber wall and walkway. Timber gateways and watchtowers were placed at intervals around this rampart. From the second century, these original ramparts were enclosed by a stone wall, about five metres high, topped by a parapet. Towers were built at intervals along the wall and at each corner. There were four gateways, including one or two larger ones, with arched entrances, wide enough for a carriage to pass through. These were flanked by guardrooms. Outside the wall were one or more V-shaped ditches.

SEE FOR YOURSELF

Among the best examples of Roman fort remains are:

1 Housesteads, Hadrian's Wall
2 Chesters, Hadrian's Wall
3 Caernarfon, Gwynedd
4 Chester, Cheshire
5 Burgh castle, Norfolk
6 Richborough castle, Kent

The fort at Gelligaer in south Wales as it may have looked in the early second century. It was defended by a wide outer ditch and earth rampart faced by a stone wall. The workshop, headquarters building, commander's residence and granary lay at the centre. The soldiers lived in six long buildings. Outside the fort was a bath-house.

26

Inside the fort

Inside the defences were several buildings of timber and stone. At the centre was the principia, or headquarters building. Next to the principia was the praetorium, where the garrison commander lived.

Other buildings included a granary, workshop, hospital, stables and living quarters for the soldiers. There was a communal toilet for the troops, like the one at Housesteads (right).

Saxon shore forts

In the fourth century the Romans built a string of forts to defend south-eastern Britain against Saxon invaders. These had massive stone walls, nearly three metres thick at the base and around five metres high, with projecting round towers called bastions. One of the best examples of these shore forts is Burgh castle (below).

This is the toilet in Housesteads Fort on Hadrian's Wall. Stone channels ran down the middle of the room. Instead of toilet paper, the soldiers used sponges dipped into the water that flowed along these channels.

The inner core of the walls of Burgh castle in Norfolk was made from flint held together by mortar (sand and lime).

HADRIAN'S WALL

Hadrian's Wall is the most famous structure of Roman Britain. It was built between 122 and 136 CE, on the orders of the emperor Hadrian, to protect the northern border of Roman Britain against the independent tribes of Scotland.

Construction

The sheer scale of the project was extraordinary. The wall was about four metres high and a maximum of three metres wide. In the picture above you can see that the inner part is rougher looking than the smooth outer parts. This is because the builders used shaped stone for the outside of the wall only, filling the middle with a mixture of rubble and a cement made from clay, sand, lime and water. This method allowed them to build the wall very quickly.

Around 3.7 million tonnes of stone were used in the wall's construction, all from local quarries. The wall ran for 118 kilometres from the Solway Firth in Cumbria on the west coast, through Carlisle, to the east coast at Newcastle-upon-Tyne.

Milecastles were fortified gateways, controlling movement through the wall. Each milecastle usually contained two barrack buildings for troops.

Defences

At every Roman mile along the wall was a small fort, known as a milecastle. Milecastles were built above arched gateways in the wall, like the one pictured above, and could accommodate about a dozen soldiers each. Milecastles helped soldiers to control the movement of people across the frontier.

At regular intervals between each milecastle were two turrets, enabling soldiers to keep watch over every section of the long border. Further defences were provided by ditches to the north and south of the wall like the one pictured below.

PAST TO PRESENT

Over the centuries much of the stone from Hadrian's Wall was reused in other local buildings, including monasteries at Jarrow, Monkwearmouth and Lindisfarne in Northumberland. This continued until the early 20th century when the wall was frequently used as a source of building material for roads and field walls. In 1987 Hadrian's Wall was granted protected status as a World Heritage Site.

To the north of the wall was a deep V-shaped ditch, as shown here. The ditch made it difficult to cross the wall at any point other than a milecastle or fort.

41 CE Claudius becomes the fourth Roman Emperor.

43 Roman armies invade southern Britain.

44 Colchester captured.

48–60 Romans conquer Wales.

49 Colchester becomes the first Roman capital city.

54 Emperor Claudius dies.

84 Romans conquer the Scottish lowlands.

117 Hadrian becomes the 14th Roman Emperor.

122–127 On the Emperor Hadrian's orders the Roman army builds a wall across northern England from the River Tyne to the Solway Firth.

138 Emperor Hadrian dies.

139–142 Romans build the Antonine Wall across southern Scotland from the Firth of Forth to the River Clyde.

163 Romans abandon the Antonine Wall and withdraw south to Hadrian's Wall.

197 London becomes the new capital and soon a wall and gates are built around the city.

275 Shore forts are built on the south and east coasts as a defence against people from northern Europe.

324 Christianity becomes the official religion of the Roman Empire.

366–367 Attackers from Scotland, Ireland and northern Europe join together to raid as far south as London but are driven back beyond Hadrian's Wall.

400 Romans abandon Hadrian's Wall.

410 Roman armies leave Britain.

altar a table or flat-topped block used as a focus for religious worship, especially for making offerings or sacrifices to a god or goddess.

amphitheatre an oval arena surrounded by rising tiers of seats.

archaeology the study of ancient civilisations by digging for their remains and examining them.

draper someone who sells fabric and sewing materials.

flue a shaft used as an outlet for smoke from a furnace.

garrison troops stationed at a military post.

glazed fitted with glass.

granary a storeroom for grain.

mosaic a design made from small pieces of coloured stone.

parapet a low, protective wall at the edge of a platform. Defenders would fire their weapons over the parapet.

polygonal with three or more straight sides.

portico a covered entrance to a large building consisting of a roof supported by pillars.

province a country or region controlled by the Roman Empire.

rampart a defensive fortification made of an earth embankment often topped by a low wall.

trellised surrounded by an arched lattice of wood used to support plants.

vault an arched structure that forms a ceiling or roof.

veranda a porch, usually roofed, that extends along the outside wall of a building.

villa a country house in the Roman Empire with living quarters and farm buildings.

World Heritage Site a site chosen by UNESCO (United Nations Educational, Scientific and Cultural Organization) for special care and preservation.

Bignor Villa, West Sussex
www.romansinsussex.co.uk/sussex/bignor.asp
Bases of the walls and beautiful mosaics survive.

Brading Villa, Isle of Wight
www.bradingromanvilla.org.uk
A Roman-British farm with surviving mosaics.

Caerleon Fort, Amphitheatre and Baths,
Newport (type 'Caerleon' in 'search site')
www.cadw.wales.gov.uk
Fortress town with barracks where soldiers lived,
baths and a spectacular amphitheatre.

Caerwent, Monmouthshire
www.cadw.wales.gov.uk (type 'Caerwent' in
'search site')
A Roman town with fourth-century walls,
forum-basilica and a Roman-British temple.

Chester Roman Amphitheatre, Cheshire
www.english-heritage.org.uk (type 'Chester'
in 'Search')
An archaeological project is unearthing
information about this amphitheatre.

Colchester Castle Museum, Essex
www.colchestermuseums.org.uk
Displays many Roman objects found locally.

Corinium Museum, Cirencester, Gloucestershire
www.cirencester.co.uk/coriniummuseum
Shows what Roman rooms and shops looked like.

Fishbourne Roman Palace, West Sussex
www.sussexpast.co.uk
Has the largest collection of mosaics remaining
in a Roman building in Britain and a garden.

Hadrian's Wall, Cumbria and Northumberland
www.english-heritage.org.uk (+search)
Coast-to-coast wall across northern England
with watchtowers, forts and the temple of
Mithras at Carrawburgh. There is a museum
at Vindolanda Roman fort.

Leicester Jewry Wall
www.leicestermuseums.ac.uk/museums/
museframe.html
A 9-metre high wall, which was part of the
exercise hall at a bath-house. It is next to the
Jewry Wall Museum.

Lullingstone Villa, Kent
www.english-heritage.org.uk (+search)
Has a hypocaust, wall paintings and mosaics.

Museum of London
www.museumoflondon.org.uk/english
Has replicas of Roman shops and the inside of a
Roman house as well as Roman coins, jewellery
and sculptures from the temple of Mithras.

Painted House, Dover
cka.moon-demon.co.uk/painted.htm
Town house remains with painted wall panels.

Roman Baths, Bath, Somerset
www.romanbaths.co.uk
One of the largest Roman baths in Europe.

St Albans, Hertfordshire
www.stalbansmuseums.org.uk/
verulamium_museum.htm
Town with Roman theatre, a mosaic floor and
town walls as well as the Verulamium Museum.

**Silchester Roman City Walls and
Amphitheatre,** Hampshire
www.english-heritage.org.uk/server/show/
conProperty.215
The best preserved Roman town walls in Britain.

Wall (Letocetum) Roman Site, Staffordshire
www.english-heritage.org.uk (+search)
Remains of a staging post, foundations of an inn
and a bath-house with a site museum.

Wroxeter Roman City, Shropshire
www.english-heritage.org.uk (+search)
Excavated centre of a large Roman city.

INDEX